THE NEW BEATRICE

OR

THE VIRTUE THAT COUNSELS

THE NEW BEATRICE
OR
THE VIRTUE THAT COUNSELS

A Study in Dante

BY

GRATIA EATON BALDWIN

New York
COLUMBIA UNIVERSITY PRESS
1928

INTRODUCTION

The task I have set myself of finding the meaning hidden behind Dante's symbols has been a labor bringing with it great joy; for in its course a new world of thought has been opened to my understanding, revealing to me a spiritual activity transcending experience and defying expression. It is this spiritual faculty that I see figured in Beatrice, "the glorious lady of Dante's mind." If, in trying to develop this idea, my study tends to be more affective than speculative, it is designedly so; for I hope by this treatment to make the poet's philosophy more intelligible to the unlearned reader. I have been moved, too, by the thought that in departing from Latin, the vehicle of all speculative writings of his time, to his beloved mother tongue, the poet was not only urging the cause of the vernacular, but seeking the friendship of all who used this "lowly and unstudied speech, such as is used by women." If this essay can win for him another friend, a friend in that high sense which he taught, one inspired by sincere love, with no thought of profit or advantage, or if it can stimulate those who have been arrested by the beauty of the letter to dis-

3

cern the far more excellent beauty of the spirit, it will be justified.

Although I feel somewhat rueful in adding one more interpretation to a number already manifold, it has been, I must confess, this very multiplicity of readings that has confirmed my belief that the truth was yet to be found. For my presumption, however, I am most humbly apologetic in trying to compass within this brief space an elucidation of a work which was the outcome of ten years of unremitting toil and which "had been blessed by both heaven and earth." But my own zeal, kindled by the thought of my great master's eagerness to convey to an erring world his vision of the truth, has emboldened me to share with my fellow students the ray of light which has fallen to me. Meanwhile I study, as did he, to write of this Beatrice more worthily; and I pray, as was his prayer at the close of the *Vita Nuova*, that, if it pleases Him through whom all things have their being, that my life may endure a few years longer, I, too, may say of her "what has never been said of any woman."

The verification of this interpretation has been made difficult by the obscurity of early records. Although the year of the poet's birth is sufficiently authenticated, the month in which it occurred has

4

to be determined solely by his reference in the *Divina Commedia* to his first breathing the Tuscan air when the sun was in the constellation of Gemini. That he was baptised in his beautiful San Giovanni we have also only from internal evidence. Without further documentation this thesis may seem to the rational mind based largely on evidence unseen. Although, to give stability to my proof, I can fall back upon the argument that Dante disclaimed any autobiographical intent, asserting that his subject was " *homo,*" I am hoping to find favor with those who can discern, what I hold as belief, that the thought of this essay has been directed by " the virtue that counsels."

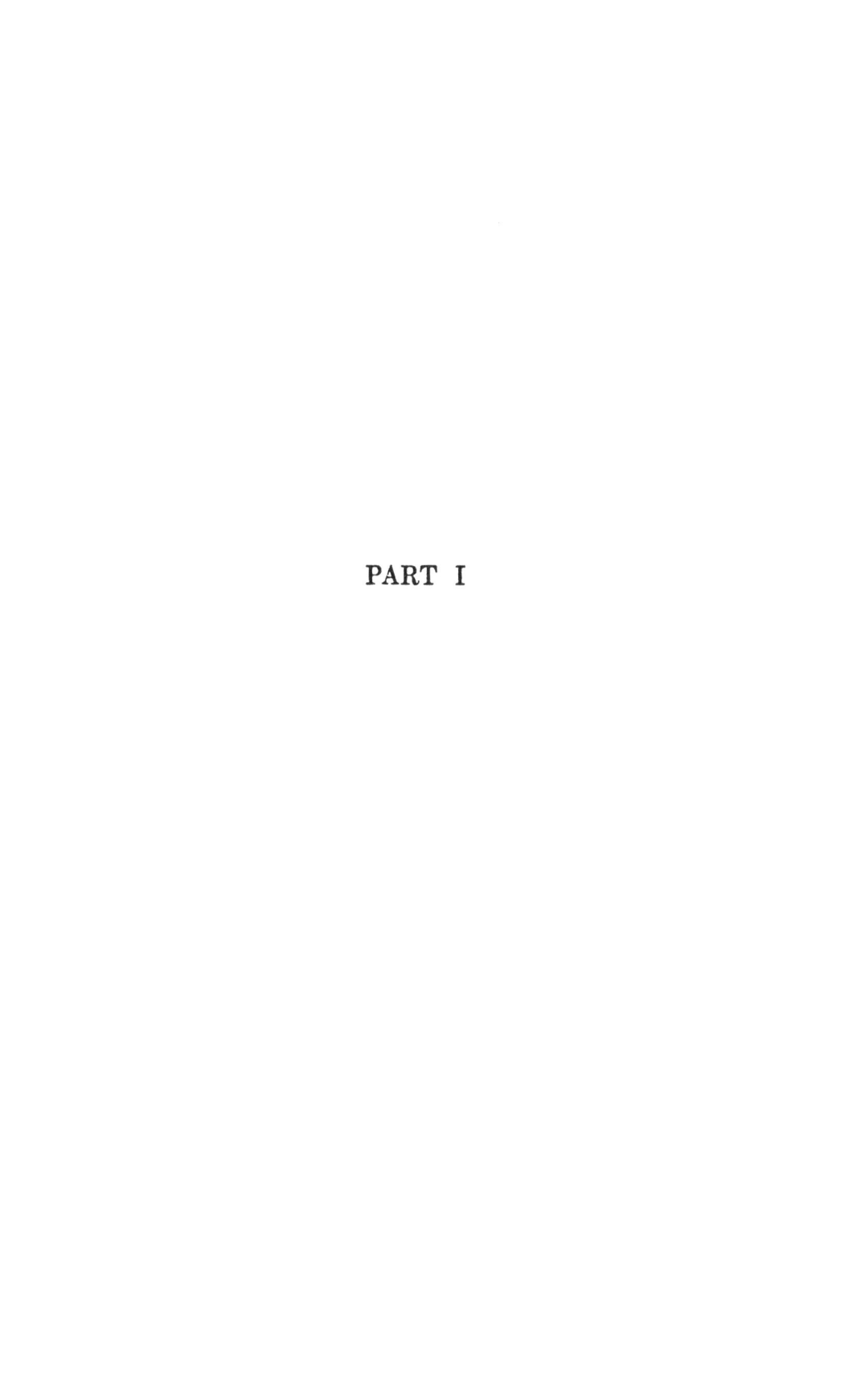

PART I

Seeking consolation for the loss of the first delight of his soul, "the most noble Beatrice," Dante relates in the *Convivio,* he sought the schools of theology and the disputation of the philosophers and found in the demonstrations of truth revealed in the eyes of The Lady Philosophy a remedy for his tears. With a purpose not unlike, several years ago I entered a class in the study of Dante, and I likewise in seeking silver found gold; for while the exercise of my mind brought solace to a sorrowing heart, the poet's enlightened faith ennobled and illumined a faith that was blind.

I recall a day when the class discussion fell upon the significance of Beatrice. We passed over many of the allegorical meanings that commentators had seen masked by the guise of a woman: faith, grace, charity, theology, favored by so many medieval writers, wisdom and his own soul. These and others we applied, but without conviction. Willing to accept the word of the leader of our thought, who was to his pupils "a sea of all learning," that she was some aspect of wisdom or truth, which, though obscure to us, was without a shadow of doubt perfectly defined in the poet's mind, we were unwilling to give up our belief in his early attachment to a visible woman, who only after death became subtilized into a reality of the supra-sensuous life. I also recall resenting a statement made by a fellow student that it would be impossible ever to discover the real meaning of Beatrice, so remote and dissimilar to our own were the poet's life and thought. If it is truth, I argued always to myself, for I was inarticulate from distrust of my own judgments, although man's vision of it may change, it is the same yesterday, today, and forever. Up to this time my reasoning had been the reasoning of others. Ever to learn seemed the preoccupation of those about me, and I did not question its high worth. Not even the possibility of coming to a knowledge of truth had occurred to me till it came to me in that class discussion and begat in me an ardor that has carried me on through doubt and misgiving to a vision from which my eyes never turn save to return with fuller confidence.

I began at once my enterprise. Isolating from the context all the terms with which the poet invokes the Lady of Virtue called by many " Beatrice, who knew not what to call her," I surveyed them alongside of the apostrophes to Wisdom found in the Old Testament. Dante's " Beloved

10

of the first lover" instantly called to mind the words of Solomon: " I loved her and sought her out from my youth. I desired to make her my spouse, and I was a lover of her beauty . . . yea, the Lord of all things Himself loved her." The poet exalts her as a " Splendor of living light eternal." Solomon sings, " For she is the brightness of the everlasting light, unspotted mirror of the majesty of God." Here was similarity, but not identity; for such phrases as " She who imparadises my mind ", " My celestial escort ", " That beatitude, the end of all my desires ", seemed to suggest that her ministrations were to Dante's individual soul. This idea gained greater precision from Virgil's words, " Truly in regard to so deep a doubt, decide thou not till she tell thee, who shall be a light between the truth and the intellect."

Pondering these appellations so spiritual in import, and her alleged identity with the mystic number nine whose root was the Blessed Trinity, as well as the many suggestions of resemblance between her virtue and the " Power and Wisdom that opened the way between heaven and earth," no other than " the Word that took flesh and dwelt among us," I began to recoil from any idea of love of even the memory of a woman of flesh and blood.

11

The New Beatrice

It was at this point that I turned to question the authority for the existence of an historical Beatrice. And what did I find? That all this romantic love story that had touched the hearts and stirred the imaginations of men for so many centuries was based on the words of Boccaccio! It seems that nearly half a century after the events recorded, Boccaccio had written a short treatise in praise of Dante in which he relates the events of the poet's life, plainly taken from Dante's own works, identifying Beatrice with a certain Beatrice Portinari, the date of whose birth, marriage and death seemed to be in accord with the vague details set forth with such mysterious implications in the *Vita Nuova.*. Although this information has the further support of Peter Alighieri, the son of the poet, in a rewriting of his own early commentary, the fact that no mention of a Portinari is made in that first codex, nor in the most brilliant of the early commentators like Jacopo della Lana and the Ottimo, taken together with the testimony of Buti, coming soon after Boccaccio, that Beatrice was but a creation of the poet's fancy, must surely weaken the cause of the partisans of an historical Beatrice. We must be mindful too, that the art of Boccaccio was narration; and, though I have no desire to question his erudition or to discredit his admiration for the poet, to the spiritually minded he must be classed with those whom the poet regarded as having the habit of knowledge, without knowing how to operate with it, since inclination was ever binding their understanding. Critics have already found other misstatements made by the author of the *Decameron*. That he showed greater discernment in his letters is evidenced by a passage in which he states that Dante's are no foolish rhymes, but that their hidden meaning is deeper than their outward covering. To add to these arguments there was the failure of the chroniclers such as Villani, Pucci and Bruni to make mention of a Portinari.

Notwithstanding all this opposing testimony, this legend has found favor with a large class of readers, and I was of this number. It was only a careful study of the *Convivio* that dislodged it from my mind. Here Dante pleads to be exempt from all imputations of a love for delight of the senses, averring that his love was for truth and virtue. The word virtue, it must be noted, had a far deeper significance than modern usage conveys, carrying to the schoolmen an idea of a spiritual or intellectual activity of the soul. Again and again in his discourse he calls the literal meaning false and the allegorical true, insisting that his

13

usage is that of the poets, who by this rhetorical
device conceal the truth under a beautiful lie.
In the *Vita Nuova* he again denounces all the
poets who are not able, when called upon, to
denude their work of its garb of figure and disclose its real import. Does he not intimate, fur-
thermore, in the *De Vulgari Eloquentia* that,
while others write of love and war, he writes of
rectitude and the guidance of the will?

Then there is another argument eloquent in
its appeal to the idealist. After proclaiming that
his second love recalls his first, he disclosed by
intricate dialectic that this second love, The Lady
Philosophy, whose soul is love and whose body is
wisdom, is no other than the essence of God himself. Could there be any comparison between
this stupendous idea and Beatrice, unless she too
was from the beginning a pure idea? There was
still another enlightening detail; her years are
counted in the *Vita Nuova* by the slower move-
ment of the starry heaven, which, we are told in
the *Convivio*, signifies only things metaphysical
and incorruptible. To cap this proof there is her
name Beatrice, one who makes blest, so appropriate to the highest and the holiest virtue. As I
bent over the pages of the *Convivio*, its high purpose to serve as a key to unlock the gates of

14

the allegorical operated in me. One by one the props which had upheld my belief in an earthly love fell before its teachings. I felt immeasurably freer.

All this while there was growing in my mind a fuller appreciation of the value of the symbol to depict the psychic forces which are the chief agents in the development of character, and whose action and interaction make up the drama of man's mental life. The validity of this mode of expression, extolled by theologians as well as by poets of all ages and races, has its basis in its analogy to the processes of reasoned knowledge, advancing, as it does, according to the schoolmen, from the cognition of sense impressions into a world of abstract and universal ideas. In justification of this method of instruction, often so cryptic that the mind of man has failed to probe beneath its surface, medieval theologians offered reasons physical as well as metaphysical. Nature herself had kept many of her secrets even from the most favored of her children. Arguing from the teaching of the Prophets as well as from Aristotle, they regarded the world as a book, written without to the carnal or earthly man, within to the spiritually minded. Although, as was reaffirmed by St. Paul's teaching, it was possi-

15

ble to get a knowledge of the hidden things of God from the phenomena of sense, it was reserved for the Author of the book Himself to reveal its true meaning in a divinely instituted way. " The Wisdom that came down from heaven" was looked upon as the "precious pearl" which was hidden always to those who were lost, only darkly seen by many, but revealed as living knowledge to the faithful who sought it with a pure heart.

Thus allegory with its address to flesh as well as to spirit soon became a method. The occult presentation of truth became an art assiduously cultivated by poet and philosopher; but while the latter seemed to comprehend the verity of both literal and allegorical, the poet, whose name, Dante records, lasts longest and is most honored, made the literal serve as a beautiful mantle to conceal the truth. That this latter mode, to Dante's thinking, bore greater similitude to the relationship of the visible to the invisible world, a profounder study of his philosophy must disclose.

The mind of the student of today, with its passion for rapid transit even in passing from the world of sense to the world of thought, finds this system of instruction clumsy and often baffling. Especially is this the case with the English-speaking thinker with his restricted use of the feminine

16

gender; for even personification finds less ready access to his mind. Dante's world, on the other hand, was a world of figuration. He could behold all about him the figures of women vivid in fresco or pallid in stone, betokening by gesture or demeanor the virtue or vice they embodied. Doubtless his first acquaintance with the Seven Liberal Arts, in the study of which even in his boyhood, Boccaccio tells us, he made such marvelous advance, was made through their human semblances painted or chiseled on wall and façade. In literature likewise these personified abstractions became the *personae* of drama and tale, and the theme of the poet's amorous verse. Not only in literature were they delineated, but the Lady Philosophy spoke from profound works of theologians; and no less a metaphysician than St. Augustine illustrated the subtle distinction between will and free-will by a lady looking at a window, and a lady looking at a passer-by through a window.

Knowing that the schoolmen had subjected consciousness to a complete analysis, and assigned to each faculty of the soul distinct and appropriate activities, I now sought to identify Beatrice with the highest of these operations.

Since some knowledge of the questions under discussion in the schools, arising from the applica-

tion of Aristotle's teaching to Christian doctrine,
is necessary to an understanding of my thesis, I
will try to outline the one that has the greatest
bearing. According to the teaching of the Master
Aristotle, *being* presupposed two elements, potentiality and actuality. In the sensible world there
was always a *materia* disposed to receive and an
active principle or *forma* which made the thing
what it was. With the acquisition of this formal
element came an activity which caused the *materia*
to pass from a state of potentiality into act. In
the world of thought there was an analogous relationship; for the possible intellect, infused by
God at or near birth, was regarded as susceptible
of union or identification of itself with truth,
while the active intellect effected this modification.
Whether these were two separate activities of the
soul, or two aspects of the same faculty were im-
portant questions in the schools; but a theme of
far greater moment, one, indeed, which threatened
to disrupt Christianity itself, was the theory
sponsored by Averroes, the great commentator of
Aristotle, based on his master's characterization
of this intelligence as "separate, impassible and
imperishable." From this word "separate"
issued a new philosophy opposed to all the funda-
mental doctrines of the Church. If this intelli-

gence was a universal principle, as Averroes taught, one for all men, acting as an agent apart from the soul, by participation in which man was able to know all truth, then personal immortality, free-will, the justice of rewards and punishments were meaningless terms. Hell, purgatory and paradise were but the vain imaginings of a frenzied prophet's fancy. The foundations of the faith were shaken. Against this heterodoxy was waged a warfare that engaged the thoughts and energies of the leaders of theology for many years, even centuries. No more zealous antagonist was to be found than the Dominican brother, St. Thomas, who, making use of the same arguments as his adversaries, employed them with the acumen of a master logician to destroy the system which was subverting the doctrines of the order to which he had consecrated his life and thought. The force of his dialectic quelled the contention for a while, but it was constantly being rekindled in the schools. So insensate did hostility to the great commentator become that Dante was judged harshly by many critics for his leniency in placing him in Limbo beside his master Aristotle, and for assigning to Sigier of Brabant, known to be a follower of his teaching, a place among the learned doctors in Paradise.

How the mind comes into possession of purely conceptual knowledge has always been a problem to the philosophers. The history of human thought, as well as man's individual experience throughout all ages, has attested the fact that it is possible for the human mind to attain a consciousness in which pure concepts have a reality more living and more quickening than the realities revealed by sense impressions; nay more, as holy schoolmen taught, and none with more persuasive eloquence than their poet disciple, Dante, the mind aided by divine grace could aspire in this temporal world to a vision of the Truth which is the principle of all being and unity and freedom. To overcome all opposition of the flesh, so that the mind, set free from the phantoms of the imagination, could exist, as it were, outside of itself as a *materia* to a sole agent, God, and hear words ineffable, because incapable of transmission through the instrumentality of a corporeal organ, was not a hypothesis of philosophic speculation, but a fact realized in the consciousness of the individual. The reality of this experience who can call into question, who heeds the instruction of St. Paul or of Dante?

Although in the poet's time a large class of thinkers, embracing the Epicureans who formed so appalling a number that Dante devised for them a special section in Hell, denied the existence of conceptual knowledge save as refined products of sense, the followers of the faith accepted the solution given by St. Thomas, which was based on the tenets of Aristotle. In accordance with his system, knowledge was first through the senses; but since, as was also posited, no spiritual accident could be the outcome of a material agent, there must be in man a spiritual cause producing a spiritual effect. This was no other than the possible intellect existing not apart from man, but separate because not operating through any bodily organ. The method of transition from purely empirical knowledge, the object of sense, to the intelligible, the object of the intellect, even as developed by the ablest of logicians, Thomas Aquinas, taxes the understanding. But from the enlightenment given by Aristotle, the student may gather that the possible intellect was a mental state in which these concepts were only virtually present. Its purpose was to serve as a treasure house of ideas. "To make them actually present," said the Master, " as colors in a dark closet need light to make them actually visible, there must be an active principle to make these universals really operate in man."

For greater illumination we must turn to the
Divina Commedia. In the *Purgatorio* Statius explains to Dante how from an animal the foetus
becomes a speaking being — "As soon as the ar-
ticulation of the brain is perfect," he says, "the
Primal Motor turns with joy to this work of
nature and inspires a new spirit replete with
virtue, which draws what there it finds active into
its own substance, and, making one single soul,
lives and feels and on itself revolves." This is
the possible or potential intellect, which, as Dante
further instructs us in the *De Monarchia,* is the
specific characteristic of the species man. Differing from the brutes below who have only a faculty of apprehension; differing from those fully
actualized creatures above, "than whom man is
but a little lower," he alone is distinguished by the
potentiality of his intellect. It is possible for man
alone to go downward toward the brutes or upward toward the angels.

Others had sought to assimilate Beatrice with
the *intellectus agens,* or active intellect, which the
Master depicted as "the illuminator of the human
mind, making him more than man, even divine":
but there came at once to oppose this theory in
my mind the fact that nowhere in his works does
the poet refer to an active intellect. To upper

and lower, speculative and practical, he alludes;
but these seemed designated by the reason and the
higher consciousness that revolved upon itself,
but was itself in potentiality to a higher *forma*.

Inasmuch as my thought had already allied
Beatrice with some mystery hidden in Jesus Christ,
I now directed my study to find some counterpart
to this activity whose merit would be more especially the theme of the theologians. In the search
which followed I found my mind constantly re-
verting to the striking explanation of free-will
found in the first book of the *De Monarchia* and
again in almost the same wording in the *Paradiso*,
" The greatest gift," are Dante's words, " God bestowed upon human nature, most conformed to
His goodness and most pleasing to Him; " for by
it, he adds in the former work, " we reach happiness here as men and blessedness there as gods."
The analogy between this faculty and the active
intellect caused me to reflect. Beatrice, too, had
the same high office. Indeed, all that was predi-
cated of her could be attributed to this greatest
gift to men. The insistence of this idea of concurrence, and the flood of light it cast on many
perplexing problems in his works urged me to
greater endeavor.

I at once gathered together all the passages re-

ferring to *liberum arbitrium* or free-will. There
was first the speech of Marco Lombardo in the six-
teenth canto of the *Purgatorio*. It is not necessary
to consult the pages of history to learn the condition of the world at the beginning of the four-
teenth century. The poet's pages ring with indig-
nant sorrow for the wickedness of his fellow men.
The world was " running unto death." Even the
Church was " astray in acquisition of gold."
" Blind Covetousness " had bewitched the hearts
of his people. Addressing Marco, he says, " The
world is utterly deserted by every virtue and with
iniquity is big and covered. I pray that thou
point out to me the cause, so that I may see and
show it to others, for one puts it in the heavens
and one here below."

" Brother, the world is blind," was the reply, " and
thou, it seems, comest from it. You who are living
refer every cause upward to the heavens as if they of
necessity moved all things. If this were so, *liberum
arbitrium* would be destroyed in you, and there would
be no justice in having grief for ill, or joy for good.
The heavens initiate your movements. I say not all,
but granted that I say it, light for good and evil is
given you and free volition which, if it endure fatigue
with its first battle with the heavens, then conquers all
if well it is nurtured. To a better nature, though free,
you are subject. And that creates the mind in you

24

which the heavens have not in charge. Wherefore, if the present world do go astray, the cause is in you; be it sought in you."

Again in his letter to the Italian Cardinals the poet inveighs against the tendency of men to attribute to necessity what by an ill use of their freedom of will they have preferred of their own choice. Marco then goes on to picture the soul as issuing from the hand of Him who delights in it even before it is.

"It knows nothing save that, moved by a glad maker, it turns to that which gives it pleasure. Of trivial good at first it tastes the savor; then, deceived by this, it evermore runs after it, if guide and bridle bend not its love. Wherefore it was necessary to have laws for a curb, and a king that at least could discern the tower of the true city. The laws exist; but who puts hand to them? Not one, because the shepherd who precedes has knowledge of what is right, but fails to operate with it; for, following pleasure, he seeks only material good, and the people, seeing their guide aim only at that which they covet, feed on this and seek no further."

The need of right leadership was a cause which inflamed the poet's soul. It was *la mala condotta,* he avers, "that makes the world blind, and not human nature that in man may be corrupted."

25

"Rome," Marco continues, "which once made the
world good, was wont to have two suns that made visible both the one road and the other, that of the world
and that of God. Now the sword is joined to the cro-
zier, and they must of necessity go ill; wherefore,
through corrupting in itself two modes of rule the
Church of Rome has fallen in the mire and defiled
itself and its burden."

It was the instruction of Virgil, however, that
filled me with higher hope. In the seventeenth
canto of the *Purgatorio* the famous sage discourses
about love. "Neither Creator nor creature ever
was without love, either natural or rational. The
natural is always without error, but the other may
err either through an evil object, or through too
much or too little vigor." "While love," he continues, "is directed upon the primal goods and on
the second moderates itself, it cannot be the cause
of ill delight; but when it is bent to evil, or runs to
good with more zeal or less than it ought, against
the Creator works his own creature." His pupil's
thirsting mind is not yet satisfied; he wishes to
learn the nature of this love, to which his Master
refers every good act and its contrary. Virgil, in
reply, admonishes him to beware of the blind who
make themselves leaders. "The Soul," he says,
"which is created disposed to love is mobile to

26

everything that pleases it as soon as by pleasure it is aroused to action. Your faculty of apprehension draws an image from a real existence and displays it within you, so that it makes the soul turn to it, and if, thus turned, it inclines to it, that inclination is love. It is nature which is bound anew in you by pleasure. Then the captured soul enters into longing, which is a spiritual motion and never rests till the beloved make it rejoice. "Now," he concludes, "it may be clear to you how far the truth is hidden from those who aver that all love is a laudable thing, because perchance its matter may be good; but not every seal is good though the wax be good."

Dante's mind is tormented by doubts. If loves are offered man from without, and always under the aspect of good, for the schools taught that nothing could attract the will save under the aspect of good, how can man be held blameworthy if he goes crooked, provided he sin not in the above-mentioned ways. Dante argues: if it is natural for the soul to love, and love is not bent to evil in hatred or malice and runs not to excess or deficiency, how can there be a question of merit or demerit in heaven, when reason sees that these loves are determined by the conditions of an external world?

27

The New Beatrice

The answer to Dante's questions is so precious to my theme that I must give it in full:

"So much as reason seeth here I can tell thee. Beyond that, wait for Beatrice; for it is a work of faith. Every substantial *forma* that is separate from matter and is united with it has the virtue of the species residing in it, which without action is not perceived nor shows itself save by its effect, as by green leaves the life in a plant. Yet whence the intelligence of the first cognition comes man doth not know, nor whence the affection of the first object of desire which exists in you even as zeal in the bee for making honey; and this first will admits not desert of praise or blame. Now in order that to this every other may be gathered, the virtue that counsels is innate in you, and must keep the threshold of assent. This is the principle wherefrom is derived the reason of desert in you according as it gathers in and winnows out good and evil loves. Those who in reasoning went to the foundation took note of this innate liberty; wherefore they bequeathed morals to the world. Assuming that every love kindled within you arises of necessity, there is power in you to restrain it. By this noble virtue Beatrice understands free-will; and therefore see that thou have it in mind, if she take to speaking of it with thee."

Virgil's words, "Wait for Beatrice, for it is a work of faith," taken with the preceding words of Marco, "To a better nature, though free, ye are

28

subject, and that creates the mind in you," opened to my thought new vistas.

There was much to ponder in the word *intendere*. This word, signifying to understand, was pregnant with meaning in the schools. "*La nobile virtu Beatrice intende per lo libero arbitrio.*" The motive powers of heaven, named by the common people angels, and represented with hands and feet to condescend, the poet explains, to the capacity of man who first sees through the senses what later is made worthy of intellect, controlled by understanding (*intendendo*) the revolutions of the spheres. God *understood* in the sense of giving existence to primitive matter, that unknown and unknowable substratum of all things.

If Beatrice was an activity of his soul, I reflected, she must of necessity understand her own act. She must be in control by thought of this innate principle of liberty. That she was some high *forma*, or at least the specific virtue gathered therein, seemed evident. She manifested herself by her counseling power; and his gain in clearness of vision and firmness of purpose, as she led him from glory unto glory, was plainly the effect of her exalted teaching. Indeed, no part could be assigned to her that so well defined her function in the *Divina Commedia* as that of winnowing out

all evil and gathering all good loves into the
one sovereign desire of his heart for his Creator.
In the *Convivio* we are told that man desires with
all possible longing *to be,* and since his being
comes from God and is preserved by Him, the soul
desires and wills to be united with God so that his
own being may be fortified. It needed but little
further reflection to discern not only that this
operation was ordained to be man's highest act,
but that if, as Dante affirmed, the highest aim of
man was to exercise to the full the possible intellect, then man was destined to become the product
of his own highest activity. As I called to mind
the Philosopher's maxim, " Man's highest operation denominates the man," I was reminded of
several passages in the *Paradiso* in which Dante
appears to use " counsels " to designate the deni-
zens of the celestial spheres.

The poet's idea of reasoned knowledge was in
accord with the teaching of the schools. " Reason
following the senses has short wings," we find him
saying. Thomas Aquinas, whose thought, the
poet hints, Beatrice's most resembles, affirmed that
because the reason could come to many sides of a
conclusion, most of the errors in thought arose in
the progress of the mind from premise to conclusion. He therefore posited in man a superior

faculty of vision which, similar to the intuitive wisdom of God, could see all things at a glance. We may infer from Virgil's words that it was the part of reason to see its own limitations. The sphere of its activity was over the functions adapted to man's perishable end. All empirical knowledge and sciences derived therefrom were its contribution to philosophic thought; and how high a value Dante put upon this terrestrial glory may be noted by his reverence for Virgil, who typified it, and by the grief at his disappearance, even though he already discerned, but not perfectly, the spiritual glory that excelleth. Observing obedience to law in the phenomena of earth and heaven, the reason could instill lessons of humility and submission to a Sovereign Being whose likeness was imprinted by His instrument nature on the visible universe. Man is a product of man and the sun, maintained Aristotle, " the master of human reason." If teachers and guides, together with the accidents of parentage and environment, largely the outcome of the heavens, were influential in determining man's loves, the reason could perceive the injustice of a doctrine of rewards and punishments unless there was innate in man a higher light to discriminate among its own diverse judgments and discern the difference between the

31

good and the apparent good. Reason should be lord of the sensitive will of man. It could bring back into rectitude the will that was bent to evil in envy, hatred or malice. Knowing the mean, it could prod the will that was slack, or curb inordinate desire for material good; but the soul of man entered into longing that was a spiritual motion and passed beyond reason's ken. From this fact alone man could argue for the existence of a higher light.

My opinion was already gathering certitude. There was added to strengthen conviction, Dante's exposition of his work presented in his letter to Can Grande. After setting forth the theory of the complex meaning of the *Divine Comedy*, he states that the subject of the whole work, according to the letter, is the state of souls after death; according to the allegorical point of view, the subject is man according as by his merit or demerit, in the exercise of his free-will, he is deserving of reward or punishment by justice.

My first insight into this theory of the meaning of Beatrice assured me that her significance was the same in the *Vita Nuova* as in the *Divina Commedia*. It was therefore with some delight that I came upon The Sonnet to Cino da Pistoja in which he relates that, " since the circling sun his ninth year closed, he had passed his days in fellowship with love, and that reason and virtue had been as one who piped amid the storm, and *Liberum Arbitrium* had been in danger of his darts, and counsel's shafts had sped in vain." The fact that in the *Vita Nuova* Beatrice first appeared to him towards the close of his ninth year indicated, it seemed to me, that this record of the struggle between flesh and spirit anticipated the larger treatment it received in the *Vita Nuova,* and that this in turn forecast its fuller development in the *Divina Commedia.* Interpreted in the light of this foreword, the first vision in the *Vita Nuova,* whose meaning was long dark even to his *fedeli d'amore,* that group of elect poet souls whose motive for being was to pose just such figurative enigmas to one another, was an allegorical treatment of the contention between love, a faculty bound by nature, and the intellect, a purely spiritual activity. Here he depicts a lord of fearful aspect carrying in his arms the sleeping Beatrice, whom upon waking he forces to eat the heart he holds. Then his joy is changed to weeping and he bears away to heaven the form of Beatrice. It might well be a figurative rendering of the discussion of *liberum arbitrium* in the first book of the *De Monarchia.*

33

"If the judgment wholly moves the will (*appetitus*) and in no way is anticipated by it, then judgment is free; if on the other hand the judgment is moved by the will and in some way is anticipated by it, it cannot be free, for it does not act of itself, but is dragged captive by another." I discerned already in the death of Beatrice the loss to his soul through sin of this divine faculty of judgment. Since in the will was the seed of all unworthy as well as worthy actions, the will was ordained to be in subjection. Its dominance must perforce tend to carnalize and therefore to destroy the spiritual faculty, in which was man's beatitude and his freedom. The full nature of this freedom was not yet revealed to me; that it was a later disclosure to the poet's thought I am inclined to believe. In the last two sonnets of the *Vita Nuova*, those " pilgrim " thoughts inspired by reflection on the Veronica were the heralds of a *nuova intelligenza* which revealed itself as the very image of God in man.

Elated as I was with these results of my research, when I advanced from the consideration of my proof to an extended exposition, I was met by discouragement, even dismay. Everywhere in the poet's work I read the lesson of man's dependence upon God. The prophet's cry, " The way of man is not in himself; it is not in man to direct his steps," was not more eloquent than the poet's prayer, "Give us this day the daily manna without which, through this rough desert, he backward goes who toils most to advance." Man was but a mere potentiality; his actuality was in God. How was I to avoid the heresy of the Arabian school and yet bring this idea into harmony with man's moral freedom and personal responsibility? Beatrice's birth was not coincident with Dante's. Could she, then, be a faculty of his soul? A thousand questions surged into my mind. What was the meaning of this word *innata?* Was this virtue connatural to man in his origin? Then why was it the work of faith? And faith, we know from many oft-repeated precepts, came through one portal only. In baptism, when the soul became manifest to God, man came into the faith and was vested with the three holy virtues.

All the problems involved in any exposition of the fall and redemption of man, doctrines of grace and predestination, of the principle of individuation, and of the origin of good and evil faced me and confounded me. My inability to understand, I concluded, was due to some fault in me. Perhaps I was not receptive to the poet's light because I was not prepared to receive it. This thought became insistent as I reflected upon his words concerning friendship, that relationship which loomed so large to his eyes of peerless seeing that it stood behind the connection of letter and spirit, *materia* and *forma*, and even earth and heaven. "For the virtue of one thing," he says, " to descend upon another, the second must be brought to the likeness of the first." It was this desire to bring myself to his likeness and to understand the *Divina Commedia* in its making that set me to reading all the works which I fancied would clarify my perturbed vision. First I sought out those writers whose works had been a light to him, Boethius, Cicero, St. Augustine, Richard of St. Victor, and hosts of others, and with greater diligence those two master makers of his thought, Thomas Aquinas and Aristotle. My zeal, ardent as it was, in no way matched my master's, for I endured neither hunger nor cold nor vigils in this pursuit; but I found myself at a library desk many months, even years, always hoping for clearer insight into the complex question of man's moral freedom. I soon lost the little light I had, for the comprehension of it ever seemed to recede as I advanced. Verily a stumbling-stone and rock of offense in the path of knowledge! Small wonder that it had divided brothers and split schools since the first choice of our first parents! Although I received little light from my long incursion into the discussion of this problem, I in no way regret the happy intimacy I gained with the thought of many aspiring souls whose singleness of purpose stimulated me to higher endeavor. From time to time I would come across some instruction that would quicken my mind into assurance that it was directed aright.

My first encouragement came from Aristotle. After defining *liberum arbitrium* as " choice based on counsel," he states in the *Eudemian Ethics* that the principle of counsel is an intellectual principle higher than our intellect, namely God. Then again it was the keen reasoning of Cicero in the *De Finibus* that gave stability to my thesis. He argues: it is a mistake to make virtue consist in the act of choice, for that implies that the thing which is the ultimate good is itself choosing something else. While I was deeply moved by the ecstatic pæan of praise in which Richard of St. Victor pours out his soul to celebrate the virtue of *liberum arbitrium*, it was the utterance of St. Augustine, " man by abusing free-will loses both himself and it ", that helped to crystallize my own thought.

The first idea that I was able to disengage from

the divergent thoughts of men was that much of
the confusion had arisen from using *liberum arbitrium* (free judgment) interchangeably with
libera voluntas (free will), notwithstanding that
the schoolmen were unequivocal in discriminating
between the cognitive or intellectual and the con-
ative or appetitive operation of the soul. Another
error seemed to arise from regarding mobility or
flexibility, even corruptibility, as freedom. As
Dante expounded in the *De Monarchia, liberum
arbitrium* could be interpreted as "a free judgment concerning will." As he set it forth, we
might even conclude that it must be a freedom
from will. There he asserts that this principle
of our liberty is a liberty of judgment which
many have on their lips, but few in their intellects.
No more forceful argument has been advanced
for this intellectual freedom than the one con-
cluding this discourse. Accepting the doctrines of
St. Thomas that God and subsistent intelligences
or angels have free-will, he adds, "Hence it is
manifest, that the angels and souls departed from
this life, whose wills are immutable, do not lose
freedom on account of this immutability, but re-
tain it in the greatest perfection and power." St.
Thomas, the "angelic doctor," always upholding
the cause of the intellect, defines *liberum arbitrium*

as a self-determination of judgment. "Only," he asserts, "when the understanding can reflect upon its own act can there be free judgment. If man is to determine himself to judge, he must act upon some higher idea or *forma*, to wit the universal idea. But, since no action follows the cognition of universals alone," he continues, "there must be a particular application of it. He must advert to himself as the author and agent of the act." It is apparent from St. Thomas's arguments that for a man to be the free agent of his moral acts the power of will must be the servant of the power of thought. There must be such a coöperation between will and intellect that man acts as a unit. Given the infirmity of sin that Christian theologians perceived in the will, was this possible to attain? Pagan as well as Christian moralists, and none with greater persuasion than St. Paul, have taken note of the strife that was ever going on in human nature, and seen in it a condition inimical to freedom. Aristotle in his ethics views the man that possesses knowledge and fails to operate with it as one blind or asleep; for he has the knowledge of the universal, but not that of the particular. "The incontinent man," he avers, "and even the penitent are not friends of themselves; for their will is at variance with their reason. They are blind; for they know what is right, but do not act in accordance with right judgment."

For a more penetrating analysis of this question we must again refer to Dante's logic made vivid by living symbols. Back of all his thought was this dominating idea, "where strife is a possibility, there must be judgment; for," he syllogised, "there can be no imperfection without a perfecting agent." Upon this basic principle he reared the splendid structures of his two master works, the *Divina Commedia* and the *De Monarchia*. In the soul of man the imperfection of his dual nature of flesh and spirit was brought to perfection by making both subject to the divine virtue of counsel. In regard to the temporal world his arguments are analogous. Between two or more princes, he states, of equal rank holding no allegiance to each other, controversy is sure to arise for which judgment is necessary. This judgment must be found in one ultimate prince of wider jurisdiction who may govern all within the circle of his right. The poet saw likewise the harmonious relationship of Church and State depending upon their allegiance to divine Wisdom "that mightily and sweetly ordereth all things," each to its separate end. The peace he sought with such unflagging zeal from world to world was based upon this principle of undivided sovereignty. Liberty in the temporal world is " the free passage from will to act, which the laws make possible for those who obey them." Liberty in the spiritual world is the free passage from thought to act, which the virtue of counsel makes possible when it holds the threshold of assent. To substantiate his thesis Dante called upon authority human as well as divine. The stirring words of Lucan, quoted in the *De Monarchia,* that the Roman world could suffer no two in command, as well as passages from Boethius and Virgil, confirmed his idea of one universal princedom. The basis of his philosophic arguments could be found in a favorite precept of the schools: " for a thing to be incorruptible, it must be in potentiality to one *forma* only." Then from the Scriptures he adduced " that saying of infallible truth, ' every kingdom divided against itself shall be laid waste.' "

My task was now to learn more about the word " counsel." Although it was often glossed " freewill " by medieval writers, it was commonly associated with one of the seven gifts of the Holy Spirit, which, according to the prophet Isaiah, rested upon " The Root of Jesse " who was to come to judge mankind, "not with the sight of his eyes nor with the hearing of his ears, but with righteousness and truth." These gifts, it was taught, were bestowed upon those who through baptism became fellow heirs with Christ. St. Thomas gives a very full discussion of this virtue, assigning to it a wider range of activity than any other intellectual operation. Insight into the past, present and future seemed to be within its range. Not only did its meaning convey the idea of sharing wisdom with another; it also suggested the action of a *forma* whose intent must always be to unfold its own likeness on the *materia*. Its connection with love was also to be marked. Love seemed both to precede and to follow it. Judgment might seem harsh, but never counsel. All this suggested analogy with Beatrice; but a far more striking parallel was to be found in its attitude of gently removing doubts. "Soothing," are St. Thomas's words, "pre-existing doubts." Too numerous to mention are the times she dispels the doubts and answers the troubled queries of his mind which only in the truth can find rest. The word was reminiscent always of its primitive meaning of reconciliation, for its manifest purpose was to reconcile the wisdom of man to the wisdom of God. Beatrice was again coming into the glory I was always seeking for her; for in the light of Scripture she now appeared as the work of a faith that overcometh all error in the gentle manner of Him who was its great pattern and exemplar, of Him whom the prophet foreknew as the "Wonderful, Counsellor, the Prince of Peace," who was to know how to refuse evil and choose the good.

My study thus far has shown that free-will is not a choice based on counsel, but a choice submitted to counsel. The agent is not a will preferring good to evil. The agent is an intellect, illuminated and actualized by truth, instilling its power into the will. It is the giving up of a false freedom for a true. It is the joyful surrender of a faculty which may lead to death to a vision which leads to truth and life. Man's freedom is not in knowing that, although he embraced the good, he could have followed evil. His freedom is rather in knowing that in that power of choice is his bondage. Man cannot establish his own righteousness, for his righteousness is in being subject to God. If there is an alternative, there must be doubt. If there is opposition, then is he twain. Man is free only when he is one.

PART II

Fuller elucidation of this solution demands its application to the allegory of the *Divina Commedia*. The reader can then determine whether it works or not.

At the opening of the poem Dante pictured himself as having lost the right way in a dark forest. Similarly, St. Augustine in his treatise on the *Utility of Believing* viewed himself as bemused in a forest of unbelief from which there seemed to be no exit. The poet, like his first father, has lost the way of truth, but not yet his life; for the first dispensation was of "one offense unto condemnation," but in the second "the free gift is of many offenses unto justification." When he is about to abandon hope, for three sins, typified by three terrifying beasts, beset his soul and press him back in affright where the "sun is silent," Virgil appears to him and renews in him the hope of ascending the delectable mountain "which is the source of every joy."

Dante conceives the reason as the first agent in bringing the will of a sinner back to the path of rectitude. Only the will disciplined by the knowledge of experience can be held worthy of a

47

higher gift. But the quickening into activity of
a soul deadened by sin is largely the work of a
guide or teacher sent not without Divine inter-
vention to point the way to life and light. The
reason of the master is then begotten anew in the
mind of the pupil, and the pupil, in submitting his
will to one of wider experience, acquires some
foretaste of that fuller freedom into which he as
a Christian is to be called. Thus we find the holy
virtue which Dante's soul had lost through sin,
the Beatrice of his beatitude, moved by the charity of "her whose benignity not only succors him
who asks, but oftentimes freely foreruns the
asking," urging Virgil to go to the aid of one dear
to her who had fallen along the way. It is not
surprising that this poet should be elected to this
high office. Beloved as precursor and prophet of
Christianity by many medieval writers, esteemed
as pattern of all virtues by St. Augustine, he is
here set forth as a teacher whose ripe reason and
disciplined will, as well as matchless craft, make
him worthy to be lord and master of Dante's
feeble and irresolute soul. In some such way as
the "Wisdom which shared the glory of his father
before the world was" has been shown in holy
writ to have ministered to fallen humanity, lift-
ing man out of his fall through the mediation of

inspired prophets and teachers, Beatrice is seen to guide Dante from afar, bringing his will back to righteousness through the ministration of heavenly messengers and the Mantuan poet. The several steps in the education of his apprehension and his will have their parallels in the progress of the regeneration of the seed of Adam. So low had the poet fallen, Beatrice tells us, that all means for his salvation had failed save showing him the lost people. Estranged from the truth and almost deaf to reason, the sensitive soul has to be moved to flee from evil through fear, which, according to the sages, was the beginning of all wisdom. Under the kindly tutelage of the " glory of the Latins," whose art had been the inspiration of his own, Dante passes from Hell into Purgatory, where love of good is inflamed by a spark from Heaven.

Like the good prince of the *De Monarchia*, who so sees the end of government that without controversy he gives over his authority to one of wider jurisdiction, Virgil yields his leadership to Statius. The ill-determined character of this leadership suggests the possible intellect. The fact that he outlines to his pupil the nature of this function seems to intimate that the cognizance of this new spirit and of its high destiny is realized

in Dante's consciousness. The deference of one
poet to the other and the recognition by Statius
of his debt to Virgil throws light upon the relationship of these two faculties. "Without Virgil's
poetic art," he declares, "he would not balance
the weight of a feather." Art and science, the offspring of experience, are the prerequisites to the
reflective life of the intellect. The intellect, then,
by circling upon itself and contemplating the data
of sense, refines and transmutes it into univer-
sality; but in its content are many aspects of good
and evil. The blindness of Aristotle's man of universal knowledge alone is here recalled. At this
stage of his development he is only in a state of
receptivity to a higher light. Until the virtue
that counsels descends to assimilate all that it
finds active there to the likeness of eternal truth,
he is affected only by operations working through
material organs.

Statius is here represented as a man who through
great diligence in learning had acquired a store of
wisdom. Through knowledge based upon experience and authority he comes to the true belief
whose seed has been sown by messengers from the
heavenly realm. Because he estimated the prag-
matic value of the practices and doctrines of
Christianity superior to those of all other sects,

and found the utterance of Virgil in harmony with this belief, he comes to baptism, and thereby becomes an heir to a heavenly heritage of grace and truth.

Virgil's parting instructions mark the peak of reasoned knowledge. Man is crowned and mitred over himself. His own judgment is free, upright and sane; it would be a pity not to do its bidding, for right reason is in accord with right desire. Pleasure now may be his guide. No further can reason see. But already in Dante's intellect falls a gleam of the eternal light. Even reason hears Beatrice's voice; and another who had already seen the light tells him " though free, he is subject to a higher nature." His soul enters into desire.

Dante now passes into the Terrestrial Paradise. Many critics, following a hint conveyed by the previous vision of Rachel and Leah, have seen here symbolized the active, as in the *Paradiso* the contemplative life. Harmonizing this view with that of Richard of St. Victor, who saw in these characters the types of the affections and the reason, I have discerned here activity as it is exemplified by its exponent, the will. All the imagery, matchless in its beauty, the fair Matilda singing like a lady enamored, gathering flowers

51

red and yellow that make gay her way, likened
to the nymphs now fleeing, now seeking the sun,
suggest the soul of man mobile to what pleases
it as soon as by pleasure it is roused into activity.
Its pleasure is now righteous, for it is inspired by
Beatrice. It desires to unwill itself from the de-
ceitful world whose pleasure it had served, so
that it may be inwilled by heavenly virtue. This
righteous zeal is evidenced by contritior. No
adequate understanding of the movements of the
penitent soul here delineated can be reached
without consulting some chapters on " The Justification of the Ungodly " as it is developed by the
ablest of the schoolmen.

If a vision of the thought of the following passages somewhat different from the seeing of
others has appeared to me, its justification may
be found in its greater accord with the instruction
I have just mentioned. I have not been alone in
seeing signs of moral error. Left and right, dark
and light, crooked and straight, to indicate false
and true, have been too consistently used by the
poet to admit of any exception. In the procession
commonly accepted as The Triumph of the
Church I have detected other indications of devia-
tion from the truth.

We know that the poet's soul in the sweet sorrow of penitence is again being wed to God. The sinner is now coming into the light of truth, which shows him the difference between good and evil. From Beatrice, Virgil had said, he was to learn the story of his life. As she opens the eyes of his understanding, revealing the man to himself, he sees the doctrines that had led him from her side divested of all their false glamour of truth and disclosed in their repellent garb of evil. The confession which he makes tells us that he has gone along a way not true, following false images of good and present things with their vain delights. We have learned from Marco that he is one of a blind world following blind leaders who refer to necessity what their own wills have chosen, and we know from his own touching words that he is going upward so as not to be blind.

Behind these semblances of holy prophets, apostles, doctors and fathers of the Church, the guides and leaders of the Christian world, following the sevenfold Spirit of the Lord, that knows no other cloud than sin, the light of truth reveals the figures of the corrupt leaders of Dante's erring world following what first appeared to be seven trees of gold, but later were disclosed as candlesticks. This procession accompanies the car of the Church, whose beauty is compared here to that of the sun, "when going astray it was consumed by the prayer of the earth, when Jove in his secrecy was just." This car is drawn by a monster of two natures, to figure not the divine and the human nature of our Lord, but the fetish of all materialistic thinkers, the idol of man's own will, human nature itself. In this procession I see portrayed the "lying world," as the poet brands it, "the love of which pollutes many souls," masquerading, as it always must to court the love of man, in some guise of that real world which alone can be the object of true love. " Only the eternal light of truth as it is seen by the intellect," he tells us, " can kindle true love; and if some other thing seduce love, it is naught but some ill-recognized vestige of the truth that therein shines through." Before Dante, as before every child of God, is life or death. Whichever he shall choose will be given to him: the way of the world, or the way of God. The choice must be his own act.

Four and twenty elders lead the procession robed in white and crowned with fleurs-de-lys. At that time there were four and twenty Cardinals, eighteen of whom were French. Only one other time does Dante mention this emblematic flower, and then to identify it with Philip the Fair when "in His Vicar he made Christ a captive." To throw more light upon this interpretation I cite a passage from his impassioned letter to the Italian Cardinals.

"But you who are the centurions of the first rank of the Church Militant, neglecting to guide the chariot of the Spouse of the Crucified along the track which lay before you, have gone astray not otherwise than the false charioteer, Phaeton; and you whose duty it was to enlighten the flock that followed you through the forest in its pilgrimage here below have brought it along with yourselves to the verge of the precipice; nor do I cite examples for your emulation, seeing you turn your back, not your face, to the car of the Spouse."

In sympathy with this reading the four living things with six wings, taken to be symbols of the gospels, may be read as the Decretals, the study of which, the poet deplores, has taken the place of the gospel and laws of the Church, as, he adds, "can be seen from their margins." We know from his own words that his world was a victim to a plague of heresies and pagan impiety. It is easy to infer that the faith of the poet, like that of Statius, had at one time been luke-warm from the same corrupting influence. In the fourth book of the *Convivio,* where he shows some taint of the

55

paganism for which he later beat his breast in sorrowing penitence, he has linked the three sects of the active life, the Peripatetic, Stoic, and Epicurean, in a mysterious connection with the three theological virtues of faith, hope and charity. This passage suggests an explanation of the three strange maidens at the right wheel, who have been commonly regarded as these three holy virtues. Since Dante has presented these pagan sects as the guardians of corruptible things, it would seem consistent with my reading to find them here seducing the world under the aspect of the virtues which were the guardians of the incorruptible. Surely the four arrayed in purple led by one with three eyes in her head could be no other than the four vices which St. Thomas represents as counterfeiting virtues, especially as he describes " prudence of the flesh " as tripartite in accordance with a text from St. James's Epistle.

A passage from the *Paradiso* disclosed to me the reality of the following figures, " one showing himself a disciple of the great Hippocrates, the other of contrary concern." The eulogy of the saintly athlete Dominic reads: "not for love of the world, for which men now fash themselves, following the Ostian and Thaddeus, but for love of the true manna, he acquired learning." The former was a noted jurist and the latter a famous physician of that time often called by the Florentines Hippocrates. Both were denounced by the poet as distorters of truth. Coming behind the next group of four, abject in appearance, is seen an old man with a countenance of keenness, walking as one asleep. I hope it is no vain vision that discerns in this solitary figure the image of the great poet himself, going along the way that was not true, pursuing false images of good. Old he was in suffering, and old in the sense that the natural man which the penitent puts off is always old to the new. Perhaps he is here withdrawing from a servile band to make himself a party by himself, as Cacciaguida foresees him and as the red on their brows might indicate; and perhaps it is that grave concern of poverty consequent upon his exile which, he sadly pleads, has been so bitter and so hindering, that has helped to darken the eyes of his mind.

"When grace descends," instructs St. Thomas, "vices are withdrawn and virtue infused." We can imagine such a change taking place here. For when Beatrice appears in a cloud of flowers above the chariot, the ancient virtue that had transfixed him ere he was out of boyhood, smote him through and through. He turns to the stream, and as he sees himself therein, his brow becomes heavy with shame. Every step reveals the action of this work of faith. When he reads in Beatrice's eyes the difference between good and evil, so pricks his heart the nettle of repentance that what had most turned him aside to its love became most hateful to him. As Matilda draws him through the stream Lethe, purging his soul of the consciousness of sin, his condition recalls the estate of our first parents. Reason has advised obedience to God's law. The intellect longs for its perfection; but the will, though free from sin, is still bound to pleasure by nature. Although the mouth of Beatrice has been unveiled and he is persuaded, for " the smile of Wisdom," the *Convivio* tells us, " is her persuasion," the truth is not yet operative in his soul, for he has not yet freely given himself to it. The judgments of Beatrice here seem harsh and cruel. The fault, we may infer from the *Convivio*, is in him.

No penitence can be accounted sufficient unless the penitent call to mind the work of redemption and meditate upon the mystery of the Incarnation. He must weigh with devotion all the blessings this sacrifice brings to mankind and how he by the sacraments is made a partaker of these benefits. At this juncture in the *Purgatorio* the great drama of the redemption is re-enacted in Dante's mind.

When Beatrice and the seven beautiful ones lead the Gryphon to the foot of the Tree of the Knowledge of Good and Evil, and the affixing of the pole of the chariot to it causes the boughs that before were barren to flower again, the poet reviews the supreme sacrifice of the Son of God in enduring the death of the cross that man might live. They all murmur " Adam "; but perish the thought that this beast of twofold *forma* should typify our Lord Jesus Christ! Rather let it symbolize the nature he united with himself, the Adam that was and is, and is to be; not being, but the possibility of being, a contingency, either good or evil, a conflict of flesh and spirit, a principle of yea and nay, a body corrupting in itself two modes of rule. In the juxtaposition of the Gryphon and the Tree, whose boughs the wider spread the higher they rise, is shown the relationship of the first Adam to the second. This is St. Paul's " as in Adam all die, even so in Christ shall all be made alive" (*1 Cor.* 15:22). " The first man Adam was made a living soul; the last Adam was made a quickening spirit " (45). "As we have borne the image of the earthy, we shall also bear the image of the heavenly " (48).

59

The pole of the chariot with its crosspiece was commonly taken as the symbol of the cross, which according to medieval legend was taken from the Tree of Knowledge. This tree, it was also taught, had been despoiled of virtue after the sin of Adam. The restitution of the cross to the tree and the consequent flowering illustrated how Christ had brought life to mankind. He had made out of both one. By freeing the will of man from sin, he had opened the way between heaven and earth and released the truth from its long interdict; for " the truth," affirms the saintly Thomas, " is to the effect not only that good is good, but that evil is evil." This revelation, so tremendous in its power to move that its effect upon his soul is likened to that of our Lord's transfiguration upon the three, could be significant of but one great mystery, the sacrifice of the Mass. When the Gryphon withdraws and Beatrice guards alone the chariot attached to the Tree, the world is crucified to Dante and he to the world. In a world enslaved by pleasure, he seemed indeed the sole guardian of " the religion of spiritual liberty " his Lord had come to establish.

Beatrice now goes on to disclose to him all the dire consequences of the doctrines he has followed.

Evil is shown as evil stripped of all appearances of truth. Dante's intimation that from Frederick and his quarrel with the Pope came the discord of his own troubled times suggests that, in the vision called up before him, the eagle which shatters the tree, causing the chariot to reel from side to side, must be the Emperor, Frederick II, who with his gross materialism undermined the belief in the sacred mysteries of the Christian faith. Greed, chief foe of justice, symbolized by the fox, leaped into the fold, only to be put to rout by Beatrice, enemy of all sin. The emperors that followed, by abandoning the sacred trust of emperors over the Romans, left open to the Church the temporal power. Thereby the holy vehicle became a monster and then a prey to the House of France, " the evil plant which overshadowed all the Christian lands." Thus the way was paved for the removal of the Papal See to Avignon. The allegory then appears to illustrate the atrocities of Florence, the " abandoned Myrrha," as head of the Guelphic League, and her machinations with Robert of Naples to oppose the imperial progress of the God-sent Henry, whose cause was to Dante more precious than life. In his blasting letter to the Florentines, as well as in his letter to Henry VII, he details these events.

There is no more opposition in his soul. At the instance of Beatrice, Matilda, as one making another's will her own, leads him to the stream Eunoe; and from its draught he rises renewed and disposed to mount to the stars. The virtue that counsels has winnowed out all guilty loves. Dante has entered upon the glorious liberty of the children of God.

It is not within the scope of this paper to discuss the political theories of Dante. Its concern is with a metaphysical problem; but it must be plain that no theory of individuation could be developed by the poet independently of that of Christianity or nationality. His philosophy was built up on the principle of analogy. The will and the reason were the prototypes of Church and State. From a hint given in the *De Monarchia*, where he has coupled the individual prince and the one universal monarch with the practical and the speculative intellect of man, it may be inferred that the lesser and the greater prince were shadowed forth by Virgil and Statius. In the imperial power, which was received from on high and was ordained to establish, by a government common to all, the peace and freedom necessary to the well-being of the world, Dante discerned a likeness to the new spirit emanating from God which made one soul revolving upon itself. In order to perceive in Statius even an adumbration of the one universal monarch, man's temporal end must be viewed in relation to man's spiritual end. Statius is the just prince that " sees at least the tower of the true city." In comparing the speculative intellect to the one supreme prince Dante assigned to him rule and direction only in those things which are common to all. This rule the particular prince ought to receive from him as the practical intellect, receiving the major premise from the speculative, adds to it a minor premise of its own, and so proceeds to a particular practical conclusion. It is Statius who unfolds to Dante a vision of eternal things; it is Virgil who says " thine own judgment is free, upright, and sane."

The Church, in so far as it conformed to its divine ideal, the life of Christ here on earth, submitting in all things to the Wisdom and Power that was its *forma* and its spouse, was symbolized likewise by Matilda as she made of her will an oblation to Beatrice, who in a larger aspect prefigured the Word of God. The Gryphon in like manner, with its transmutations from one to another mode of rule, must have reference to the iniquitous union of Church and State. In corrupting in itself two modes of rule, the Church had gone the way of the flesh and become a daughter of Adam. Only through the Cross could the corruptible put on incorruption. Her restitution to being and unity and goodness could be effected only through repentance and humble submission to the confines which were defined for her by God himself.

No greater champion of the Roman Empire ever lived than Dante. The empire " whose arts were to teach men the way to peace, to show mercy to the subject, and to overcome the proud," and in whose " unique census the Son of God had willed to be enrolled as man," he exalted as worthy to hold the guardianship of the world. No more zealous son of the Church was ever born than he who saw that the Church was without error only as it followed the life of Christ here on earth, imitating His example and obedient to His precepts. But greater than his allegiance to State or Church was his allegiance to the truth. No timid friend of that truth, he raised his voice to proclaim a liberty which was the inheritance of each faithful child of the Church and which was subject to God alone. Regnant in the power which this " gift of freedom " brought to him, he arraigned before the tribunal of its just judgments:

"proud Christians, diseased in vision of the mind, who had confidence in backward steps," "shepherds who differed not from the idolaters save that they worshipped one idol and these a hundred," and emperors who overstepped the circle of their jurisdiction and "in blasphemy of act robbed the tree sacred to God's use alone."

Although the identity of Beatrice with the virtue of counsel seemed now to me certain, the miraculous nature of this gift of God I saw but obscurely. A greater zeal in the application of my mind to the truth "rained down upon the Scriptures Old and New," together with the working of "the living knowledge," the leaven which makes all minds one, made my theme emerge from darkness into light. With full consciousness of my insufficiency to treat of so exalted a subject, I have essayed the task. Even he to whose expression the resources of genius, art and use had contributed almost beyond the measure of man had found that his thought soared so high about this lady that the intellect could not follow.

Beatrice in her discourse presents to Dante a great doctrine. "Because he would not endure for his good any curb to the power that wills," she tells him, Adam, "in damning himself, damned all his offspring. Whereby the human

race lay sick below for many centuries till it
pleased the Word of God to descend where he, by
the sole act of his eternal love, united with himself
in person that nature which had removed itself
from its Maker." Human nature united with its
Maker, as it was created, was pure and good. Body
and soul, made without mediation by the hand of
God, were free because not subject to " new "
things. These new (in the sense of last created)
things, taught the schoolmen, were secondary
causes, inherent in the heavens; and all things in
potentiality to their action, like the souls of plants
and brutes, were perishable. But the flesh as well
as the spirit of our first parents was incorruptible
because inspired directly by the Supreme Benignity, who so enamored it of himself that it was
nevermore without desire of uniting with the
source of its being.

Beatrice states that before Adam, Noah, Moses
and Abraham none was destined for salvation.
The human nature of the first Adam and of the
last, the Son of Mary, was without blemish and
therefore receptive of all the light that human nature could receive. With the light he had, the first
father could have seen that, though free, he was
yet subject to the divine nature. Advantaged with
every advantage, there in a world of clearer vision,

where heaven and earth were obedient, like Lucifer, the first proud one, "for not awaiting light, he fell immature." "It was not tasting the tree," Adam tells Dante, "that was the cause of so long an exile, but solely the act of disobedience." Liberty was the fruit of the tree, and it was sweet to man. The desire was natural; but the first man, following a blind leader whose guide was pleasure, craved wisdom not for the holy purpose for which it was created, but for self-exaltation. Human nature as created was an equality of mind and heart, both subject to God. The outcome of the first father's disobedience was disorder. The will overstepped its measure. It now assumed command, a prerogative never designed for it. By this act of disobedience Adam "lost the way of truth and his own life." "It is sin alone," Dante tells us, "that takes away man's liberty and makes him unlike the Supreme Good so that by His light he is little illumined." The virtue of that tree could be discovered only by those who had learned humility and submission. God's compact with man has been from the beginning: "If ye love me, ye will keep my commandments, and I will come to you and will manifest myself to you." Human nature created good and for good drove itself from the Earthly Paradise. It chose

death rather than life. With flesh and spirit subject to God there was unity, and liberty and being; estranged from the Creator there was duality
and bondage and death. The flesh of man became
subject to the heavens, or secondary causes. He
was "in bondage under the elements of the
world." God's provision was fulfilled; for his children ate in sorrow of the tree all the days of their
lives, since knowledge was only through the senses
and men were ever deceived. They had liberty,
but it was a liberty of the flesh, and it drove them
from sin into greater sin. With flesh and spirit
always contending against each other, what hope
was there for man? All through the ages can be
heard the cry of mankind exiled from its proper
home. The writings of the prophets echo with
lament for a world which called good evil and evil
good. The poetry and drama of the Greeks sang
of fate, an image of their own blindness which
they blindly worshipped. Philosophy voiced in
Cicero the thought of man. " The great cause of
discord in the world," he says, " is not knowing the
difference between good and evil." Therefore men
sought wisdom; but since they in their wisdom
knew not God, their wisdom brought them greater
discord, for it was ever seeking some new thing.

Man, having sinned through Adam, had to

be reconstituted in righteousness; for of himself he could not rise. On the one hand, schooled by philosophers who had learned from nature many of her secrets, the sensitive will of man was brought under the rule of reason. On the other hand, guided by prophets and holy teachers and by the Mosaic law, the will of man was brought back to rectitude. "When the fullness of time had come," arose a woman whose will was so perfect in its humility that to all mankind it has become the ensample. The will that offered itself with the prayer "Be it unto me according to thy word" has been exalted in the heavens as the pattern of the will so denying self that grace without measure was bestowed upon it. At this time when the temporal world was blessed with universal peace and "no ministry to man's temporal happiness lacked its minister," man desired to "have life and to have it more abundantly." Human nature, not yet united with the divine but already touched with its holy effluences, found its highest expression in the son of a learned priest and holy mother, beloved child of nature, crying to a sinful world, "Repent, for the kingdom of heaven is at hand!" "He that cometh after me is preferred before me, for he was before me." The voice of the natural man hailing the advent

69

of the spiritual rang out in the wilderness of a
world of spiritual strife. "He must increase, but
I must decrease. He that cometh from above is
above all. He that is of the earth is earthly and
speaketh of the earth."

The cross was the way held out to restore man
to his entire life. "God gave himself to make
man sufficient to raise himself again." By submitting his will to the divine, by obedience even
unto death, "Jesus Christ made such satisfaction
that it overcame the balance of all sin." "He
filled up where man had made void." By the Incarnation the Word of God subsisted in human
nature made properly its own. God's eternal
counsel was given to men. The sublimity of the
theme evokes the poet's most noble utterance:
"Virgin Mother, daughter of thine own Son,
humble and exalted more than any creature, fixed
term of the Eternal Counsel, thou didst so ennoble
human nature that its own Creator disdained not
to become its own creature."

Thus our Lord became "the first-born among
many brethren"; for into the essence of this divine
and human union each individual of the species
might enter in a new and mysterious way. He
"must be born again, not of blood, nor of the will
of the flesh, nor of the will of man, but of God."

70

Each living soul, "scant receptacle though he might be" for so great a gift, could be a recipient of a share in His wisdom and His power. The early fathers of the Church made much of the gift of enlightenment that came in baptism. "A garment of wisdom," it was called, one of the twofold garments to be worn at the final judgment day spoken of by Isaiah and St. John. Although St. Thomas in no way identifies the virtue which is infused in baptism with "the virtue that counsels," his arguments in the *Contra Gentiles* clinched my own. "With the acquisition of a new *forma* comes the activity of a new virtue; but the virtue accruing in baptism is only potentially present in man; it is the sacrament of the Eucharist that makes it an operating principle in his life." This instruction brought deeper insight into the virtue conveyed by the two channels of grace symbolized by the streams Lethe and Eunoe. The former, the sacrament of penance, effaced the sins committed after baptism; the latter, the Eucharist, gave God to man. By these holy sacraments, which make the individual soul a partaker of the benefits brought to mankind by the Incarnation and death of our Lord, God had fulfilled his promise given to Abraham for his seed and those who were accounted for the seed. He had blotted

out their sins and had written his counsel in their
minds and in their hearts. Heretofore God had
been known to man through his senses. He had
been revealed by the words of his prophets. Now
came a new way. Remembering no more their
offenses, God wrote his truth in their innermost
minds. "The Wisdom that laid the foundation
of the world" had come to his own; and though
his own had received him not, "he had borne their
griefs and carried their sorrows," so that he might
share with those who received him the riches of
his wisdom and his love.

At the holy font where the poet became a
Christian under the name of Dante he was enrolled as a child of God and of the Church and an
heir of salvation. In that fellowship certain obli-
gations were entailed; for in order to share in the
heavenly gifts, which were given without measure to the first-born, he must follow Christ's example. He must die unto the world. He must
with Christ crucify the whole body of sin so that
he might rise with Him.

We know that the poet had strayed from the
right way. He had followed the way of the world
and lost Beatrice. When through contrition he
again is started on the way to salvation, it is
Beatrice that calls him by his name, which of

necessity, he tells us, is registered here, the only time it occurs in all his work. At the sound of his name he turns to Virgil; but Virgil, " his more than father," has vanished. Reason can no longer be a refuge to man when he takes up the profession of his faith. It has guided him to its portal; but passing within, he comes under a new law. It is a religion of liberty and a life of grace. It is this new life that I believe to be figured by the *Vita Nuova.* Beatrice was only a potentiality till the later sacrament, doubtless his first Communion, when she became known to him. All the details of his love for her, transcending all earthly passion, and the emotional experiences detailed in these exquisite lyrics, are in harmony with the figuration of many theologians depicting the soul's communion with God. Sanctioned by St. Paul's likening Christ and his Church to spouse and bride, confirmed by the spiritual interpretation of that most amorous of songs, *The Canticles of Solomon,* the writings of the more affective theologians veiled under carnal imagery the ecstatic pleasures of the soul's union with God. The beautiful new style initiated by Dante and his poet friends, influenced by the vivid figures of religious discourse, refashioned the formal diction of the courts of love into a beautiful mantle designed

to conceal a moral or philosophic lesson. All the
terms ascribed to Beatrice and the effect her salu-
tation had upon him are similar to the beneficent
effect of " the cup of salvation." " True praise of
God," " fountain of truth," " destroyer of all vices
and queen of virtues," recall the words of Catholic
teaching extolling the benefits of this most holy
sacrament. Compare, for example, a passage from
the *Vita Nuova* with passages from *The Imitation of Christ*. From the former:

" For when she goes her way,
  Love casts a frost upon all caitiff hearts,
  So that their every thought doth freeze and perish.
  And who can bear to stay on her to look
  Will noble thing become, or else will die.
  And when one finds that he may worthy be
  To look on her, he doth his virtue prove;
  For that arrives to him which gives him health,
  And humbles him till he forgets all wrong.
  Yet hath God given her for greater grace,
  That who hath spoke with her cannot end ill.
  Love saith concerning her: ' how can it be
  That mortal thing be thus adorned, and pure?'
  Then, gazing on her, to himself he swears
  That God in her a new thing means to make."

From the latter:

" For this most high and precious sacrament is the
health of both body and soul, the medicine for all

74

spiritual languor. Hereby my vices are cured, my passions bridled, my temptation overcome, virtue begun is increased, hope strengthened, faith confirmed, and love inflamed. Of myself cold, dull and undevout, by Thee I am made fervent. . . Thou art a fountain always full and overflowing. . . Let me set my lips to this heavenly conduit.". . " For who is there that approaching humbly unto this fountain of sweetness doth not carry from thence something of its virtue? "

In baptism, Dante tells us, the soul becomes known to God. In the Eucharist God becomes known to man. The unknown and the unknowable live in him. The invisible becomes visible and the unreal real. By means of this sacrament " the living bread of righteousness and truth," " which came down from heaven to give light unto the world," becomes the life of men. Through Beatrice the mind of Christ was being formed in Dante. The truth, no longer coming according to the way of the flesh through the senses, is now innate in him. It actualizes his intellect the more as he renews his life at the holy fountain. This was the meaning of " a work of faith." " He that is born of God," the Epistle says, " overcometh the world; and this is the victory that overcometh the world, even our faith."

St. Augustine comments upon the new signifi-

cance the word *faith* assumes after the coming of
Christ. Before that time, as St. Paul affirmed,
man was shut up unto the faith which was after-
wards to be revealed. Man believed, but he could
not see what he believed. He accepted the word
of God and it was accounted unto him for righteousness. But man's will was still serving two
masters. He was blind. Our Lord by his passion
had brought back the will of man to the good
which was in the true. He had broken down the
partition between flesh and spirit. He had
destroyed the enmity between the will and the intellect, and " out of twain he had made one new
man, so making peace." Truth now illuminated
this intellect and gave to man a new gift of spiritual sight. There came a certitude of belief that
only the truth indwelling in him could give.
Man now saw what he believed. The liberty,
then, into which the Christian is called, is a participation in God's eternal counsels. Beatrice
was the measure of this gift to Dante's soul.
Given to him only potentially in baptism, it becomes an operating principle in his life as he
yields to its dominion his natural powers. Upon
its activity is founded his freedom and beatitude.
The efficacy of this divine power in man is the

theme of the *Divina Commedia* and is most fully stated in Canto XVIII of the *Paradiso*.

"And thou shouldst know that all have delight in proportion as their vision penetrates into the True in which every understanding is at rest. Hence may be seen how beatitude is founded on the act which sees, not on that which loves, which follows after. And merit, which grace and good will bring forth, is the measure of this seeing. Thus is the progress from grade to grade."

No precept of Aristotle had greater bearing upon Christian morals than the tenet, " No *forma* can inhere in its *materia* unless the *materia* is disposed thereto." The individual soul participates in the free gift only according to its power and being. First must come the perfection of the natural, then that which is spiritual. In the largess of his bounty the Heavenly Father had provided every means for the salvation of his creatures. The Wisdom of God had come to man in his own likeness to direct him aright, showing him by precept and example how to bring the will to righteousness; for without charity faith was nothing worth. It was to the men of good will that the Prince of Peace came. Some such peace must be found in their souls as fell upon the earth when

the Word of God became man. Such a peace
comes only when man sees that of himself there is
no peace; but, confident that God is and that he
should be obeyed, he reaches out with the yearn-
ing cry of all humble souls, " May the peace of thy
kingdom come to us; for, if it come not, we cannot
come to it with all our striving. As of their wills
thine angels, singing hosanna, make sacrifice to
thee, so may men make sacrifice of theirs." If
many were " weak and sickly among men and many
slept," as Dante himself had done, it was because
they had gone to the holy altar without the free
offering of their own wills. They had eaten the
" bread of the angels unworthily." For this cause,
the *Imitation* instructs, so few become inwardly
free and enlightened, because they are loth to
deny themselves. Dante recognized the justice of
God's interdict upon the Tree. It was to show
man that he was not yet worthy, since he had not
yet learned obedience. And the interdict has re-
mained for those who come without examining
themselves and without charity in their hearts.
Though, as Dante tells us, " our Father withholds
the bread from none," " he that eateth and drinketh unworthily," says St. Paul, " eateth and
drinketh damnation to himself, not discerning the
Lord's body."

THE NEW BEATRICE

In the *Paradiso* will becomes thought, and the life principle of that thought is the virtue from on high. Reason is effaced. Imagination and memory are in abeyance. Surveying all the content of Dante's mind rich in knowledge which the long labor of study and searching reason had brought to it, Beatrice rejects what is not consonant with the truth upon which her eyes are turned, and what is reconcilable to it she retains. As she removes the doubts that had dimmed his vision, he sees that these doubts are but the provision of beneficent nature, put at the foot of truth to urge him on from height to height. The poet in portraying his exaltation in beholding the increasing splendor of her eyes and smiles is conveying something profounder than the method of the true philosopher in the *Convivio,* who not only contemplates the truth but contemplates his own contemplation and delights in the beauty of his own beholding. Here is rather " the miracle in act "; for the truth is making Dante free. The eternal things which had existed only in belief now offer to him the sight of themselves. Not supernatural is this world, but natural to him by his new birthright. " So natural was the ascent of the mind to this heavenly kingdom," Beatrice tells him, " that no more could he wonder at it

than at a stream, if from a high mountain it
descend to its base." The life of the intellect
depicted in the *Paradiso* is unlike the contemplative life presented in theology, so removed
from all concerns of the world. No cord nor ordi-
nation, to the poet's thinking, could of itself secure
this life to men. Only through the profession of
the heart was it attained, and the way was open
to all. He who by his own act took upon himself the fulfillment of his baptismal vows entered
into a brotherhood more enduring than time and
more all-embracing than the visible universe.
Dante had renounced the world only as his master.
He was no longer of the world; but he was for the
world even to the end. The counsel which was
given to him incited him, as it did the prophets
of old, to sound a warning cry to his beloved people who were going out of the way, " for the leaders of the people caused them to err, and they
that are led of them are destroyed."

As Beatrice leads him from sphere to sphere,
she unfolds to him many of the doctrines expounded by St. Thomas Aquinas in the *Contra
Gentiles*. To one which sustains my thesis I must
allude. " In the mode of vision," says the Angelic Doctor, " there appear diverse grades of
glory among the blessed. In respect to the object

of the vision their glory is the same." He concludes: "All men desire to attain to a likeness of
God, but the end corresponds to the means taken
to gain it." In the *Paradiso* all those whose vows
were neglected or made void in some part are
shown in the sphere of the moon, "only to give
sign," Beatrice explains, "of the celestial condition that has least height, for the souls of all make
beautiful the first circle." She goes on to explain
that the failure of their vows was due to the fact
that their wills were not entire. Since a firm and
steadfast will follows vision, and comes only when
man's own will becomes ready servant to the virtue that counsels, it must mean that they had not
come into perfect liberty, for their oblation was
not entire. This accords with the words of Virgil that Beatrice was "the Lady of Virtue whereby
the human species surpassed all contained in the
smallest circle."

According to Dante's philosophy, and his
philosophy was now becoming one with his faith,
only the good in proportion as it was understood
could kindle true love. The prophets of old had
foretold a King and Law-giver who was to come to
show man the way of understanding, to open blind
eyes, and to bring man out of the prison house
of the world of flesh; Dante, the new prophet,

made even the voice of reason declare that if
those grave philosophers in Limbo could have
known everything, there was no need for Mary to
have given birth. The Son of Mary had come to
quicken man's love by showing him the truth.
He had come to show him the difference between
the false seeing of man's bodily eyes and the clear
vision of the eyes of the mind.

Although Dante's ardor increases with his vision, the supremacy of the intellect in the *Paradiso*
is unchallenged by the will till he is well advanced in understanding. Only twice is the glory
of Beatrice eclipsed. Once in the sphere of the
sun, where he meets the refulgent group of those
whose wisdom had made more luminous his own,
"so disposed was his heart to devotion, and so
ready was he to give his love to God that Beatrice
was eclipsed in oblivion." Again in the highest
sphere, when he gazes upon the splendor of St.
John, the glory of this example of holy love ob-
scures Beatrice and quenches his sight. To St.
John's questions testing his love, the poet replies
in thrilling words which tell us that the work of
faith is almost done.

"All the goads that make the heart turn to God
have been concurrent to my charity. The existence of
the world and my own existence and the death that He

endured that I might live, and that which all the faithful hope for, even as I do, to-gether with this living knowledge, have brought me from the sea of perverted love and set me on the shores of the right."

Here again, after the leap of the will to exaltation, Beatrice returns to drive the motes from his eyes, "as judgment comes to one suddenly awakening from sleep."

To conform to this idea that the affections follow the act of conceiving, the Thomists concluded that the intellect of man as executive instrument reached the term first, while the will as motive power went on to the end; "for the object of the intellect," tersely argues St. Thomas, "is the truth which is in itself, but the object of the will is the good which is outside itself, but in the intellect." It is obvious that some such idea Dante wished to convey by his symbolism here; for when he reaches the empyrean, the heaven full of love and light, he turns to see Beatrice and beholds in her stead an old man. St. Bernard tells him he has been sent to terminate desire. None more fitting to enact the part than this type of living charity who so burned with desire to see the Queen of Heaven that his wish was heard and answered. He had come to figure the love which follows the vision, just as the Holy Spirit had

followed Wisdom, showing the fullness of the will
that knows no let nor hindrance, for it is em-
powered by the Supreme Wisdom. Thus upon
the affections of man working through imagination and memory the seal of God's love was imprinted, as upon his intellect was the seal of his
Eternal Counsel.

The goal of all mystic contemplation is some
kind of union with God. Even the speculative
mind of St. Thomas defined a state of rapture,
first of intellect, then of will, whereby man trans-
cended the natural faculties of his soul and became cognizant of God without the concurrence
of the imagination. In this state man was caught
up into heaven, "and knew not," like St. Paul,
"whether in the body or out of the body." Although there were varying opinions as to whether
this vision was direct and immediate, or as in a
mirror and obscure, or wholly intellectual, or an
act of the will, all seem to be unanimous that the
phenomenon was a union with the divinity of
Christ alone. His humanity ceased to figure, for
that was the object of man's sensible love. Even
St. Bernard, whose sermons overflow with love for
the humanity of Christ, saw in this supreme act
the union of the individual soul with the Word
itself. The love of the " Word made flesh " was

a ladder, as he termed it, by which man could mount to this wholly spiritual experience. It was in this sense that he interpreted the text of St. Paul: — " Wherefore henceforth know we no man after the flesh; yea though we have known Jesus Christ after the flesh, yet now henceforth know we Him no more."

As a problem of metaphysical analysis this state of exaltation was regarded as the consummation of the abstractive powers of the intellect. In this state the intellect was raised to its highest power and could become cognizant of its own essence apart from its own existence. It could see that essence in relation to the divine essence of whose light it was but a ray. St. Augustine ascribed to the soul in exaltation a vision of its own word or idea as it existed in the mind of God. Others saw it as what the soul would be, and therefore what it could be; for, the Thomistic philosopher insisted, there could be no desire without means of its own fulfillment. That Dante was illustrating some aspect of this question can be gathered from his discussion in the letter to Can Grande. There he presents it as an experience open to all; and, to disarm the cavillers who would disparage his own claim to have attained such a height, he pleads that, " he who made the sun to shine on the good and evil, sometimes in compassion for their conversion, manifests his glory even unto evil-doers."

When Dante looks up into the high heaven and beholds Beatrice enthroned there in the place her merit had allotted her, high among those whose faith had made them whole, he is imaging not only this philosophical problem, but a doctrine more in harmony with the simplicity that is in Jesus Christ, who is "the author and the finisher of our faith." Exalted in the heaven was the triumph of his own vision; "it had overcome the world." There was his intellect fully actualized by its highest operation, "the virtue that counsels." "No child of the Church," Beatrice tells St. James, "had greater hope than he;" and by his own defining hope was the sure expectation of future glory which comes from grace and preceding merit. There, verily, was the substance of the thing hoped for, and the evidence of the thing not unseen, but now seen. As with the faith of him who so saw what he believed that he walked upon the sea and entered first into the sepulchre, he beholds the truth undimmed by sin. Bold in his confidence, "for it is part of grace," assures St. Thomas, "to know that you have it," he sees the crown bestowed in heaven

which a world, given to carnal seeing, had with-
held on earth. To the principle of his liberty and
the very measure of his likeness to his Creator, he
addresses a prayer of ecstasy:

> "O Lady, in whom my hope is strong, who
> didst endure for my salvation to leave thy foot-
> prints in hell, of all the things that I have seen
> from thy power and goodness, I acknowledge the
> grace and virtue. Thou hast led me from slavery
> into liberty by all the ways and means in thy
> power. Guard thou in me thine own magnificence,
> so that my soul, which thou hast made whole, may
> acceptably to thee be loosed from the body."

The work of faith had gathered all good
loves into the one impelling desire of his heart
for God. The rapture of his will follows that of
the intellect; and in one flash he feels the ecstasy
of the full vision, while his desire and his will are
moved by the love that moves the sun and stars.
Love had now come into its own. It was free because fixed upon the good which was in the true.
In the loving use of his wisdom, which was a part
of the great body of Wisdom with which the
Supreme Love was united in eternal wedlock, his
philosophy came into the kingdom prepared, from
all eternity, for all true lovers of wisdom. Dante
had seen what he believed, and as he believed he

spoke; and, though he spoke with the tongues of men and of angels, it was with a charity which outmatched his vision, for it was augmented by a grace " which distills from a font so deep that creature never pushed the eye far as its primal wave."

COLUMBIA UNIVERSITY PRESS

COLUMBIA UNIVERSITY

NEW YORK

———

FOREIGN AGENT

OXFORD UNIVERSITY PRESS

HUMPHREY MILFORD

AMEN HOUSE, LONDON, E.C.

Bei Fragen zur Produktsicherheit wenden Sie sich bitte an:
If you have any questions regarding product safety,
please contact:

Walter de Gruyter GmbH
Genthiner Straße 13
10785 Berlin
productsafety@degruyterbrill.com